Water
in
Art

ROSEMARY MOORE

Wayland

LOOKING AT ART

Animals in Art
Faces in Art
Food in Art
Water in Art

Looking at Art is based on *Discovering Art* by Christopher McHugh, published by Wayland (Publishers) Ltd in 1992.

Cover: top left: *The Fighting Téméraire* by Turner, National Gallery, London; top right: *Woman Bathing* by Mary Cassatt, New York Library, New York City, USA; bottom left: *The Wave* by Katsushika Hokusai, private collection, London; bottom right: *Afternoon Swimming* by David Hockney, private collection. © David Hockney 1979.

Editor: Deborah Elliott
Designer: Malcolm Walker
Cover design: Simon Balley

© 1995 Wayland (Publishers) Limited

British Library Cataloguing in Publication Data
Moore, Rosemary
 Water in Art - (Looking at Art Series)
 I. Title   II. Series
704.9437

ISBN 0-7502-1438-4

Typeset by Kudos Design, England
Printed and bound in Italy by G.Canale & C.S.p.A., Turin

KS2 Library
You have been trusted with this resource
please look after it and return on time:

below.

0 4

Don Gresswell Ltd., London, N.21   Cat. No. 1208

DG 02242/71

Contents

The power of water

These huge waves show us how strong and dangerous the sea can be. Can you see how the two fishing boats seem to be 'riding' through the waves like surfers? In the background is Mount Fuji, a famous mountain in Japan.

▼ *The Wave* by the Japanese artist Katsushika Hokusai. This print is in a private collection in London.

Niagara Falls by
Frederick Church.
This painting is in
the National Gallery
of Scotland, in
Edinburgh. ▶

In this painting of Niagara Falls, in North
America, the artist shows the tremendous
power of the water as it thunders down over
the rocks. He has made the spray look so real
that we can almost feel it on our skin.
Can you see the rainbow in the bottom
right-hand corner, made by the sun shining
through the spray?

Water in the ancient world

This picture shows a beautiful garden, with a pond full of fish and visited by wild birds. The pond is surrounded by trees, many of them bearing fruit. The painting was made to decorate the tomb of an Egyptian king, perhaps to show how lucky and rich he was when he was alive.

▲ An Egyptian wall painting from the tomb of Nebamun at Thebes, in Egypt.

The decorations on this vase show a scene from a Greek story about a hero called Odysseus. He had many adventures while voyaging around the Mediterranean Sea. Here he is, sailing home with his friends. The winged creatures above the ship are called sirens. They are singing to the sailors to try to charm them away and lead them to their death.

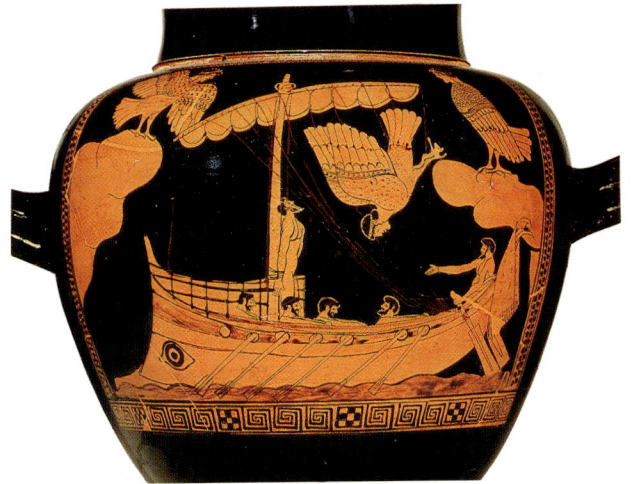

▲ *Odysseus and the sirens*. This decorated Greek vase is in the British Museum, London.

Below is a Roman picture called a mosaic. It was made with coloured stones and pieces of glass, which were stuck down. The mosaic shows fishermen and some of the many different sorts of fish that they could catch in the sea near Rome.

◄ *Fishermen in a boat.* This Roman mosaic comes from Utica in North Africa, and is now in the British Museum, London.

Water in Eastern art

More than a thousand years ago Muslim people from North Africa crossed the sea and settled in southern Spain. These people, called Moors, built castles, palaces and mosques, many of which can still be seen today. The buildings were often surrounded by beautiful gardens. One of their palaces, in the city of Granada, is called the Alhambra. This is the water garden in the grounds of the Alhambra.

◄ The water gardens, designed by the Moors, at the Alhambra Palace in Granada, Spain.

This Chinese plate is decorated with a monster swimming in the sea.

The two Indian princes (below) are greeting each other from boats on the River Ganges.

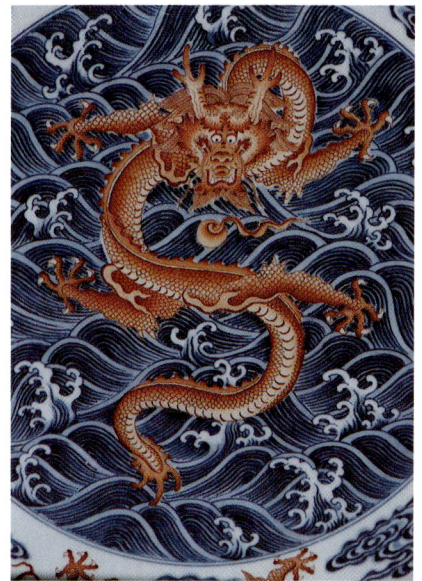

▲ A Chinese Dragon dish made in about 1730.

◀ *Princes Munim Khan and Khan Zamen in a Boat on the River Ganges.* This picture is in the Victoria and Albert Museum, London.

Water in European art

In 1066 a French prince called William of Normandy invaded England. He crossed the English Channel from France with many soldiers and horses. They landed in Sussex, where they met an English army led by King Harold. A great battle took place near the town of Hastings, and during the battle King Harold was killed. After the battle William became King William I (the Conqueror) of England. Later, a huge tapestry was made which showed scenes of these events, rather like a cartoon story.

▲ A detail from the Bayeux Tapestry. You can see it in the Museum of Bayeux, in France.

▶ A painting showing Christian ships attacking a port in the Holy Land during the Crusades.

This stained glass window shows a scene from a story in the Bible. The story is about a man called Jonah who was swallowed by a whale. Here Jonah is escaping from the whale's mouth.

The picture below shows Christian and Muslim soldiers fighting each other during the Crusades. The Crusades took place in the Middle Ages, when Christian soldiers went to the Holy Land (parts of present day Israel and Jordan) where the Muslims had settled, to try to force them to leave.

▲ A stained glass window in a church in Mulhouse, France.

▲ *The Baptism of Christ* by Piero della Francesca.

This painting, by an Italian artist, shows Jesus Christ being baptised in the waters of the River Jordan. The bird above Jesus's head is a dove, the bird of peace.

A French artist painted this picture of a seaport (below) about two hundred years after the picture of Jesus. Notice how the people and buildings look more natural than in the picture above. The men are taking stores out in little boats to the larger ships, ready for a long voyage.

▼ *Seaport with the Embarkation of St Ursula* by Claude Lorrain.

▲ *A Lady and Gentleman with Two Girls in a Garden* by Nicolas Lancret. The three pictures on these two pages are all in the National Gallery, London.

This painting is also by a French artist. It shows a family having coffee in a garden. Can you see the beautiful pond and fountains on the right? Would you say that this family was quite rich?

Mainly sea and ships

◀ *Four Day's Fight*
by Abraham Storck.
This painting is in the
National Maritime
Museum, London.

The pictures in this chapter were painted by
artists who lived in Holland and England. The
two countries were once very important
seafaring nations. The sea battle in the picture
above is being fought between the Dutch and
English. It took place in the English Channel
during a war between the two countries in the
1600s. The battle lasted for four days and was
finally won by the English.

These are Dutch people living in Holland in the 1600s. They are all having lots of fun, skating and enjoying themselves on the ice of a frozen canal. Some of them are in sledges drawn by horses.

▲ *A Winter Scene with Skaters near a Castle* by Hendrick Avercamp. It is in the National Gallery, London.

Although the painting below was made by an English artist, he has chosen to paint a scene of a moonlit harbour in Italy. Notice how he has painted the moon's reflection in the water. The moonlight makes the scene seem ghostly and mysterious.

◀ *Moonlight with a Lighthouse* by Joseph Wright of Derby. This painting is in the Tate Gallery, London.

The paintings on these two pages were made by a famous English artist who lived in London. He used to watch ships sailing up and down the River Thames, in sunshine and rain, fog and snow. His fascination with water and light is shown in many of his paintings, including *The Fighting Téméraire* (below). Turner painted this great sailing ship in harbour with a paddle steamer and other ships, all lit by a glorious sunset.

▼ *The Fighting Téméraire* by Joseph Mallord William Turner. This painting is in the National Gallery, London.

▲ *Snowstorm. Steamboat off a Harbour Mouth* by Joseph Mallord William Turner. This painting is in the Turner Collection at the Tate Gallery, London, where there is a large collection of the artist's work.

Turner painted this picture of a snowstorm at sea after he had voyaged through a terrible storm. He asked the ship's crew to tie him to the mast so that he could see, hear and feel the snow and wind, and lashing waves. Later, he described his experiences in his painting.

The Impressionist artists and water

This picture was painted by a woman artist called Berthe Morisot. She belonged to a famous group of artists called the Impressionists, who lived and painted in France in the last century. Morisot painted this picture of two friends in a boat on the River Seine, near Paris. See how she has made the water appear to shimmer in the light.

▼ *Summer's Day* by Berthe Morisot. This picture is in the National Gallery, in London.

Woman Bathing by
Mary Cassatt. This
picture is in the New
York Library, New
York City, USA. ▶

An American artist called Mary Cassatt made
this print. She spent many years working with
the Impressionists in Paris. Cassatt liked
Japanese art and she copied some of the
Japanese styles in her work. Look again at
The Wave, on page 4. Do you think Cassatt's
picture is a little like the Japanese print?

▲ *Monet Working on his Boat* by Edouard Manet. This picture is in the Alte Pinakothek, in Munich, Germany.

An Impressionist artist called Edouard Manet painted this picture of another Impressionist artist, Claude Monet, with his wife. They are on a boat on the River Seine and Monet is shown painting a river scene. Monet had this little boat fitted up as a studio because he loved to paint water and the way light is reflected on it. Manet must have thought it would be fun to paint his friends in the floating studio.

Claude Monet painted this picture of a train travelling across a bridge over the River Seine. You can see that it is quite a breezy day – notice the smoke streaming from the engine, the little scattered clouds, which almost seem to be moving, and the choppy waves of the river reflecting the light.

▼ *The Railway Bridge at Argenteuil* by Claude Monet. This painting is in the Musée d'Orsay, Paris.

This is another painting by Claude Monet,
showing the water-lily pond in his garden.
Monet used to spend hours painting the pond,
with its flowers and weeds, showing the light
on the water changing all the time. You can
visit his garden and see his pond at Giverny,
near the River Seine in France.

◀ *Nymphéas* by
Claude Monet. This
painting is in a private
collection, but other
pictures of the lily
pond are in the
Musée de l'Orangerie
in Paris.

▲ *Le Bec du Hoc, Grandcamp* by Georges Seurat. This picture is in the Tate Gallery, London.

This sea cliff in northern France was painted by an artist called Georges Seurat. He invented a special way of painting, using tiny dots of colour. He put dots of contrasting colours beside each other so that from a distance the dots – red and yellow, for instance – appear to join together to make orange. Seurat's method is rather like printing; if you look closely at a printed photograph in a magazine, you will see lots of tiny coloured dots.

Twentieth-century art

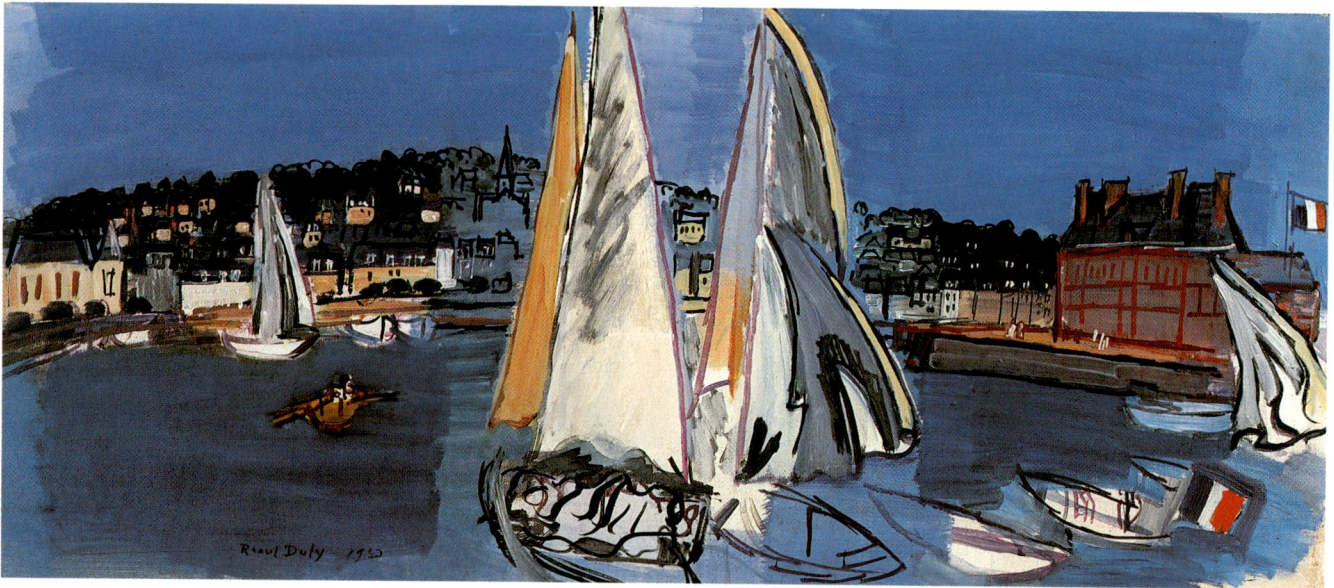

This lively picture of a busy harbour with rowing boats and yachts was painted by an artist called Raoul Dufy. Many people thought his pictures were too wild and brightly coloured. They called Dufy and his friends 'fauves', which means 'wild beasts'. Do you agree with these people?

In this picture the artist is trying to express his feelings. He has called it *The Scream*. The boy does seem to be screaming, but why? Is he screaming because he feels all alone, between the sea and the wild sky? Or because he is afraid of the two figures coming towards him? What do you feel when you look at this picture?

▲ *Sails Drying at Deauville* by Raoul Dufy. Tate Gallery, London. © DACS 1995.

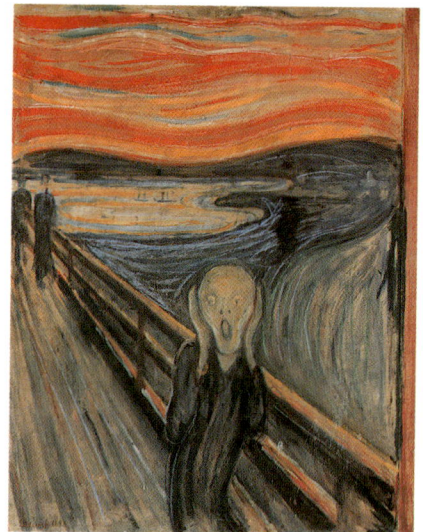

▲ *The Scream* by Edvard Munch, National Gallery, Oslo.

This picture also shows loneliness. A boy stands at the back of a ferry crossing New York harbour. He is watching the distant shore and the tugs busily chugging across the murky water. This foggy, wintry harbour scene is very different from Dufy's hot summer harbour on the opposite page. Notice how Dufy has used strong, bright colours to show hot, sunny weather, and Sloan has used dull, muddy colours for his winter scene.

▼ *The Wake of the Ferry II* by John Sloan. It is in the Phillips Collection, in Washington DC, USA.

◀ *They're Biting* by
Paul Klee. This
picture is in the Tate
Gallery, London.

In this picture, which the artist called *They're
Biting,* two people are fishing. Can you also see
the sailing boat and the lighthouse? Look at all
the fish trying not to be caught. The artist
described this picture as 'taking his pencil for a
walk'. Why do you think he said this?

This painting is called *The Waterfall.* You may not be able to see a waterfall, but maybe you can see how the picture seems to show a feeling of movement. Perhaps the artist thought that the movement was like that of falling water.

It is easy to make out the swimming pool and the swimmers in this bright, summery picture. This painting shows lots of movement too. Can you see how the swimmers' arms are thrashing the water? Do you think they are racing each other? The big splash probably means that someone has fallen in!

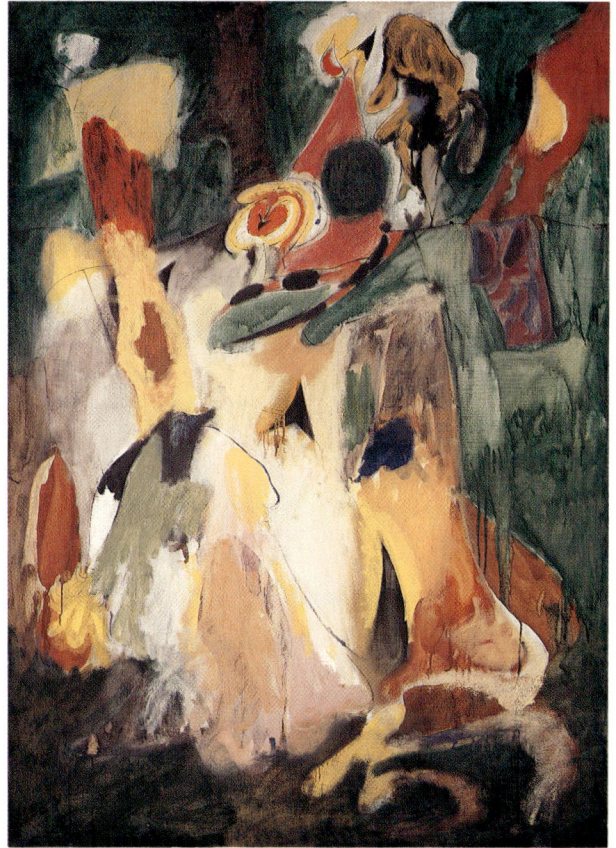

▲ *The Waterfall* by Arshile Gorky. It is in the Tate Gallery, London. © ADAGP, Paris and DACS, London 1995.

◄ *Afternoon Swimming* by David Hockney. This picture is in a private collection. © David Hockney 1979.

Who are the artists?

Hendrick Avercamp (1585-1634). This artist lived in The Netherlands and painted winter scenes and pictures of the countryside. You can see his *A Winter Scene with Skaters near a Castle* on page 15.

Mary Cassatt (1845-1926). This American artist came to live in Paris, where she became friendly with the Impressionist artists. Her print titled *Woman Bathing* is on page 19.

Frederick Edwin Church (1826-1900). Church was an American artist who enjoyed painting the magnificent landscape of North America. He belonged to a famous group of artists called the Hudson River school. You can see his *Niagara Falls* on page 5.

Claude Gellée (Lorrain) (1600-82). This famous French artist, usually known as Claude, studied in Italy, and his work was an important influence on later artists. His *Seaport with the Embarkation of Saint Ursula* is on page 12.

Raoul Dufy (1877-1953). Dufy was a French artist who enjoyed painting scenes of horse races and the seaside, in strong, bright colours. His *Sails Drying at Deauville* is on page 24.

Arshile Gorky (1904-48). Although this artist was born in Armenia, he went to live in the United States when he was a teenager. His style of work is known as Abstract Expressionism, which was especially popular in America during the 1950s. His painting *The Waterfall* is on page 27.

David Hockney (b. 1937). This British artist, who now lives in California, painted many pictures in the 1960s in the style known as 'Pop Art'. This style uses ideas and images from comics, advertisements and films. His *Afternoon Swimming* is on page 27.

Katsushika Hokusai (1760-1849). Hokusai was a Japanese artist whose beautiful prints greatly influenced the work of European painters in the nineteenth century, particularly the Impressionists. You can see his sea picture, *The Wave*, on page 4.

Paul Klee (1879-1940). Klee was a Swiss painter who did much of his work in Germany. His drawings have been described as free and 'poetic'. You can see his picture, *They're Biting*, on page 26.

Nicolas Lancret (1690-1743). Lancret was a French artist who painted pictures of wealthy people with their friends, in their homes or at leisure. His picture called *A Lady and Gentleman with Two Girls in a Garden* is on page 13.

Edouard Manet (1832-83). Manet was one of the French Impressionist artists working in Paris in the nineteenth century. Two of his most famous pictures were thought to be very shocking when they were first shown, but now most people take them for granted. His painting of his friend and fellow Impressionist Claude Monet, *Monet Working on his Boat*, is on page 20.

Claude Monet (1840-1926). Monet was the leading Impressionist artist. He was fascinated with the way light shimmers over the countryside, on buildings and especially on water. Two of his paintings, *The Railway Bridge at Argenteuil* and *Nymphéas*, are on pages 21 and 22.

Berthe Morisot (1841-95). Morisot was also a French Impressionist artist, working in Paris. She especially liked to paint family scenes and pictures with children. You can see her painting, *Summer's Day*, on page 18.

Edvard Munch (1863-1944). Munch was a Norwegian artist, who painted scenes of love, death and loneliness. *The Scream*, on page 24, is probably his most famous painting.

Piero della Francesca (c. 1420-1492). This artist worked in Italy at the beginning of a period known as the Renaissance, when many artists and sculptors produced great works of art. His picture *The Baptism of Christ* is on page 12.

Georges Seurat (1859-1891). Seurat was a French artist who developed a way of painting using scientific ideas about colour. His pictures are painted with tiny dots of colour, in a method called Divisionism (sometimes called 'Pointillism'). His painting of a sea cliff, *Le Bec du Hoc, Grandcamp*, is on page 23.

John Sloan (1871-1951). This American artist liked to paint pictures of everyday scenes showing twentieth-century city life. You can see his *The Wake of the Ferry II* on page 25.

Abraham Storck (1644-c.1708). This artist was born and lived in Amsterdam, in The Netherlands. He painted many pictures of ships and naval battles. His *Four Day's Fight* is on page 14.

Joseph Mallord William Turner (1775-1851). Turner was one of the most important of all British artists. He painted many pictures of the sea and ships. You can see two of his paintings, *The Fighting Téméraire* and *Snowstorm. Steamboat off a Harbour Mouth*, on pages 16 and 17.

Joseph Wright of Derby (1734-97). This British artist is always known by the town where he lived. He liked to paint pictures using special lighting effects, such as moonlight or candlelight. You can see his *Moonlight with a Lighthouse* on page 15.

Glossary

baptised To be immersed (bathed) or sprinkled with water, as part of a religious ceremony in the Christian Church.

Christian Someone who practises Christianity, the religion based on the teachings of Jesus Christ.

contrasting Showing a great difference.

Crusades Expeditions in the Middle Ages, when Christian soldiers travelled to the Holy Land to try to recapture the Holy Land from the Muslims.

fauves A French word meaning wild beasts. It was a name given to a group of artists early in the twentieth century, who painted pictures with strong designs and bright colours.

hero Someone who the Ancient Greeks believed to be extraordinarily strong and brave. A hero was often the son of a god.

Holy Land The ancient land of Palestine, now divided between Israel and Jordan.

Impressionists A group of artists who worked in France at the end of the nineteenth century. They were especially interested in painting the effects of sunlight.

invade To enter someone else's country as an enemy.

Middle Ages The period of time from the Norman Conquest of 1066 to about 1500.

mosaic A picture or pattern made by gluing small pieces of coloured stone or glass on to a floor or wall.

mosque A place of worship for Muslims.

Muslims People who follow the religion of Islam, taught by the Prophet Muhammad.

print A design produced by cutting out areas of a block of wood or stone to make a picture. When the block is covered with ink and pressed on to paper, the cut design is printed.

seafaring Connected with the sea and travelling on ships.

sirens Sea nymphs whose beautiful songs were believed by the Ancient Greeks to lure sailors to shipwreck and death.

studio The room in which an artist works.

tapestry A wall hanging with a picture woven into it. Tapestries were used as decorations and to help warm up the cold stone rooms of castles.

tomb A burial place.

tugs Small, powerful boats used to tow larger ships.

Books to read

The Book of Art – A Way of Seeing (Ernest Benn, 1979).
Every Picture Tells a Story by Rolf Harris (Phaidon, 1989).
Just Look . . . A Book about Paintings by Robert Cumming
   (Viking Kestrel, 1986).
Water – through the eyes of artists by Wendy and Jack Richardson
   (Macmillan, 1990).
What is Art? by Rosemary Davidson (Oxford Univerisity Press, 1993).

About the pictures in this book

Of course, all the pictures in this book are photographs. Some, like the Greek vase on page 7 or the picture of the water gardens on page 8, show exactly how the artist or architect wanted them to look (although a great deal smaller). But remember that looking at a photograph of a painting is not the same as seeing the painting itself. If possible you should try to visit a picture gallery or museum, and look at other ways in which artists have tried to show water in their work. You could try painting a picture of water yourself, perhaps showing ships on the sea, or light reflected on water as Monet did with his pictures. Or you could make a model of ships in a harbour.

Picture acknowledgements
The publishers have attempted to contact all copyright holders of the illustrations in this title, and apologise if there have been oversights.
The photographs in this book were supplied by: Bridgeman Art Library cover (top left, bottom right and bottom left), 4, 16, 18, 20, 21, 22, 27 (lower); Sonia Halliday 11 (top); Michael Holford 6, 7 (both), 9 (lower), 10; National Gallery 12, 13 (both), 15 (top), 18; National Gallery of Scotland 5; Phillips Collection 25; Ronald Sheridan Library 9 (top); Tony Stone Worldwide 8; Tate Gallery 15 (lower), 17, 23, 24 (top), 26, 27 (top); Wayland Picture Library cover (top right), 19.
Photographs of the following paintings appear by kind permission off the copyright holders: *Sails Drying at Deauville* by Raoul Dufy, page 24 © DACS 1995; *The Waterfall* by Arshile Gorky, page 27 © ADAGP, Paris and DACS, London 1995; and *Afternoon Swimming* © D.Hockney 1979 cover (bottom right) and page 27.

Index